T0381194

CREATIONS
CROWN

DENISE SYLVIA BEKKER

Scripture quotations are taken from the New King James Version®. Copyright © 1982 by Thomas Nelson. Used by permission. All rights reserved.

Balboa Press books may be ordered through booksellers or by contacting:

Balboa Press
A Division of Hay House
1663 Liberty Drive
Bloomington, IN 47403
www.balboapress.com.au
1 (877) 407-4847

ISBN: 978-1-5043-1831-0 (sc)
ISBN: 978-1-5043-1832-7 (e)

Print information available on the last page.

Balboa Press rev. date: 06/28/2019

BALBOA
PRESS
A DIVISION OF HAY HOUSE

BIOGRAPHY

Denise Sylvia Bekker

A Prophetic Christian Writer/Poetess, whose heart is to inspire and encourage with fresh revelation, revealing the Heart of The Father and His Creation. Denise is called to the Prophetic Ministry and Intercession, and loves to scribe revealing God's Covenant Love bound in truth and wisdom. Her heart's desire is to see the Body of Christ united and awakened to move from Glory to Glory.

2 Corinthians 3:18

But we all, with unveiled face, beholding as in a mirror the glory of the Lord, are being transformed into the same image from glory to glory, just as from the Lord, the Spirit.

FOREWORD

We serve a God who is very creative and it is wonderful to see some of that creativity expressed through the beauty of poetry. Denise has a real gift to write poems as she is led by the Holy Spirit. She has written some for our church which have been a blessing to many. We know that you will be blessed by reading them and experience both the love and creativity of our Heavenly Father.

Cliff Cherry
Pastor Redemption Point Church, New Zealand

ODE TO DENISE SYLVIA BEKKER

The fountain murmurs quietly,
in the rose garden in the sun.
A haven of serenity
where I relax when work is done.
Inhale the perfume thankfully
It serves to calm my troubled mind.
This is a special place to me.

By Ivor E Hogg

CREATION'S CROWN

Dancing golden sunlight,
colourful prisms of light.
Revelator of divine insight,
shining celestial ring.

Serenading dreamy moonlight,
lovers pure delight.
Creation's beauty of the night.
halo of stars unto her sing.

Twinkling stars, shining magical sight,
Constellation, diamonds of the night.
Shining hues of silver and white,
Surely God breathed them into being.

The sun, moon and stars,
Heavenly hosts from on high.
Kingdoms celestial marriage.
Greater and lesser light.

Creations Crown is nigh

Isaiah 62 v 3
You will be a glorious crown in the LORD's hand, and a royal diadem in the palm of your God's hand.

POETRY MY BRUSH

If poetry was a brush
And my words were my paint
Let your mind be your eyes
Let the strokes of my words feed your soul

Of soaring eagles, circling, watching
Over white tipped mountains, towering
Standing proud, with valleys at their feet
With lush green tree tops looking up in awe

Cold clear water from melted snow
Falling over waterfalls, moving in slow
motion
Winding rivers that carve the earth
Pushing forward to feed the ocean

Beautiful sunrise as it peeps over mountain
tops
Giving warm rays of light, feeding all
Clouds full of rain, shower life to every grain
of sand
A golden sunset disappears off the horizon

Rolling desert sands that dance with the wind
Dead grains of sand teaming with life
Amazing lakes, still like glass mirror the sky
Watching the flocks of birds playing in the
breeze

Rocking waves pushing back and forth
Icebergs bobbing like ice in a glass
Vast ocean waters that swallow the sky
Ships crossing a seemingly endless void

If my words painted a picture for all to see
One painting but different to all
Each beautiful to the mind's eye
May its beauty feed your soul

PRESENCE

Glorious manifest presence!
The wind of God carries His voice.
Like seeds being dispersed, new season begun,
Blow afresh O faceted One.

His presence entwined within our sphere.
Power and authority carried on spirited wings!
The wind of God blows here and there,
mighty pivotal power, O wings of wisdom.

Out of His treasuries He blows.
Mysteries and secrets unscrolled.
Keys that unlock revelations, old and new,
Reigning Revelator, shofar of truth.

Great winnower, O discerning wind.
Breathe upon, and open the gates.
The wind of God blows where it wills,
spiritual transportation from on high.

Supernatural dimensional power,
omnipresent, He causes His wind to blow.
O brooding force, creational power.
His breath has birthed new life, dynamic
manifest glory!

Songs of Solomon 4v16

*Awake O North wind, and come O South, blow
upon my garden.
That it's spices may flow out.*

Matthew 5v8

Blessed be the pure in heat, for they will see God.

SURRENDER

Passion flower of all love
Heavenly wind overshadows
Sweet mana rains from on high
Refreshing, vitalizing enduement
Seek the one whom you love

Embracing love, saturates
The lover of my soul
Come even so, I surrender
First love has been awakened
Well of my heart has been stirred

Behold the voice of my beloved
Caressing glory overshadows
Newness of love is at hand
Green pastures caress our feet

In refreshing we lay down
Fruit of the new season begun
Your voice so sweet to my ear
Let not the fragrance be removed

It has pleased God to awaken a new love..

Psalm 46v10

He says, 'Be still, and know that I am God;
I will be exalted among the nations,
I will be exalted in the earth.'

THE WIND

There is a song within the wind,
whispering notes can be heard.
A soft touch upon your cheek.
His flow so humble and sweetly meek.

Sweet sound of love, the wind is as a dove.
Gliding softly through the air, having no worldly care.
Swirling at your feet,
kissing them softly as He does them greet.

A song of love wisps through the air,
swirling softly touching your hair.
The wind of love is my friend,
caressing my heart, I know He was sent.

He embraces me with his love.
Clothes me with his breath.
Sweet words flow deep within.
In this purity there is no sin.

The wind of God, Ruach, what an intimate embrace.
Whispers sounds of grace.
Harken and hear his voice.
For when you do, his encompassing love turns into a song of rejoice

FIRMAMENT

Upon the rampart I did stand.
Now I have seen.
The heavens set apart,
high and lifted up.
Abiding glory on high.

Open eyed, creation power,
flowing as a mantle.
Firmament on high,
Sunset spreads its wings as a fiery dove.

A holy habitation,
Firmament, a watchman.
Dawn breaks forth, light births.
The night shadow scroll, rolled back.

The heavens display itself.
Midnight, endued with power,
then the wake of the day.
Hidden beauty exposed.

The pillar of fire blazes on high
Night shadows, as a mantle.
Firmament moves as a chariot,
day and night...
Never ceasing

BUTTERFLY

In the freedom of her flight,
that of a cool morning breeze.
She spreads her wings with ease.
Caressing the summer flow,
her vision begins to grow.

High above the tree tops,
down into the meadow she drops.
Sweet morning dew sparkles.
Unto her the flowery array harkens.

Twinkling sun rays glitter like gold,
and the cycle of Life remains as it has been told.
The morning sighs with a smile.
Glistening wings, a hue of colour,
it truly does make as a wonder...

Of what God we serve, O what beauty
surrounds us in every curve.
Now upon the meadow field,
the grass ever so green.
The flowery array begins to beam,
with smiling faces they await,
as the butterfly descends, they open as a gate.

Their pollen they do display,
petals, pert and pretty in the month of May.
The union of creation, a new Life reaction.

The cycle of splendor opens the door,
upon this, God can his love pour.
Peacefully she retreats,
accomplished that which she did just greet.

High in the sky, she does fly.
Fly butterfly fly on high,
the heavens gave a great sigh

Romans 8v21

*That the creation itself will be liberated from its
bondage to decay and brought into the freedom
and glory of the children of God.*

HIS COVENANT

Worship Him from your inner heart.
His aroma proceeds His anointing.
Golden oil permeates His name,
this, His seal of presence.

Within the secret place He overshadows.
Kingdom fragrance, releases pure joy.
He loves with an everlasting love,
transforming power clothes us.

In likeness of His image, He created,
gathered us in His embrace.
Our crowns at your feet lay.
The table of Presence, ever present.

Hearken to the Beloveds call,
colour of His love resides within heart.
Radiant glory surrounds Him,
His countenance, as the sun shining in
strength.

The restorer of covenant intimacy.
We, a new creation, bearers of His name,
He meets the desires of our heart.
Come to the house of His fragrance,
the place of His choicest!

Where covenant promises begins to flow.........

Psalm 111v9

He sent redemption unto his people: he hath commanded his covenant forever: holy and reverend his name.

A LITTLE NATURE

There is a melody that can be heard
in the cool morning breeze.
Whispering with perfect ease,
whistling an early morning song.

There is a talking among the trees,
a rustling amidst the leaves.
Loving arms reaching out to one another,
awakening the spirit of the forest.

There is a bubbling river too,
a happy chattering can be heard all through.
Up upon the banks she flows,
greeting the pebbles as she goes.

There is a smiling of happy flowers,
dewy little heads, emerging from their beds.
Sleepy colourful flowers
embracing the morning showers.

There is a little honey bee,
from flower to flower, does his pollen glean.
High above the pastures so green,
O What it is, to be so free.

There is a little green frog,
down by the marshy pond.
Sitting upon a lily pod,
Croaking and a calling, amidst the fog.

All creatures great and small, the Lord God
made them all!

Psalm 96v12

Let the field and everything in them celebrate.
Then all the trees of the forest will shout for joy.

DAWN

Sleepy horizon, amber aglow.
New born day, about to show.
Fresh beginning, brand new start,
of special blessings from God; s heart.

Wake of a new day born,
Ushering in the dewy dawn.
Rosy hues, colourful skies,
breathtaking mystery here in lies.

The wonder of creation,
thoughtful in meditation.
Crown of the dawning,
opens the curtains of the morning.

Out of the shadowy sky, dawn breaks free.
Mystical beauty begins to see.
Melody of splendor spreads out wide,
harkening the new day from every side.

The royal morning gown reveals her light.
Dawn's mythical secret hails delight.
Born again, having prophetical sight.
Rhythm of life, Dawn birthed out of the night!

Dawn the Halo of New Beginnings

Proverbs 4v18

*The path of the righteous is like the morning sun,
shining ever brighter till the full light of day.*

TAPESTRY GARDEN

Tapestry Garden of the Most High
Interwoven nations unto Him cry.
To heal their brokenness
and mend their heart in wholeness.

Tapestry Garden, in harmonious unity,
God overshadows all of humanity.
Why do we wage war
when peace is always knocking at the door.

Tapestry Garden, complimenting colour variety.
Unity and one accord, our prayer for all society.
Harmony and unconditional love
so readily given from Him above.

Tapestry Garden, God's sovereign reign,
yet nations continue to plot in vain.
He makes peace at the borders,
Gates resound His awesome wonders.

Tapestry Garden, within, the wind does blow.
The soul of the nations, begins to grow.
White linen and purple, a tapestry divine,
scarlet thread of holiness, culminated, so fine.

Tapestry Garden captivates the nations.
God arises to blow on his Garden.
To release His glory upon the brotherhood
of Man,

His delight is to bless all nations with His
righteous right Hand.

Ask of Me and I will give you the nations for
your Inheritance

Psalm 22v27

*All the ends of the world shall remember and
turn to the LORD: and all the kindred of the
nations shall worship before you*

THE DOVE

Serenity divine, o pure white Dove,
quickened from heaven above.
Royal Spirit, winged on high,
celestial treasures sing and sigh.

Pure white heavenly Dove,
surely a holy gift born out of love.
Whitened pleasure of golden love.
Where can you, your sweet feet rest?
In the hearts of those you quest.

Sweet Dove clothed in velvet white,
blessed are those, in who you delight.
Around your foot, a golden band,
betrothed you are from on high and on land.

O pure Dove of peace,
in your quest you never cease.
Bestowing goodwill to all mankind,
Solace within your heart, they will find.

Worthy you are, to behold.
As precious as refined liquid gold.
You are the wings of compassion,
o pure white Dove, Holy Spirit of divine passion

Matthew 3v16

As soon as Jesus was baptized, he went up out of the water. At that moment heaven was opened, and he saw the Spirit of God descending like a dove and alighting on him.

KINGDOM OF DARKNESS

Encroaching power of darkness,
intent to seal you with a mark.
Robe of darkness,
encompassing all with deceitfulness.

The eye of the night,
phantom body, unseen, out of sight.
Grimacing shadow with intent.
Darkness, an underground allurement.

Manifest stealth,
deep in unholy wealth.
Slight, as that of a thief,
encircling, capturing grief.

Haughty, kingdom of the night.
Summons with authority and might.
Thick darkness infiltrates,
pursuing victims, strengthening its gates.

Authority birthed from a body of doom,
All who succumb enter its gloom.
Enticing power of the night,
intriguing many within sight.

Manifold crown of deceit.
The battle has been won, so retreat!
Your kingdom keys revoked, you have been
beat!

The Light of the World put darkness under
His feet.

Light enters, darkness flees!!

John 8 v 12

*When Jesus spoke again to the people, he said,
"I am the light of the world. Whoever follows
me will never walk in darkness, but will have
the light of life."*

Psalm 18v9

*He bowed the heavens and came down; thick
darkness was under his feet.*

AWAKENING

Awaken! It's the time of spring.
Unveiling beauty, delicate but bold.
Creation begins to sing,
as a 'new thing', unfolds.

New leaves, ever so green.
Trees clap their hands!
Happy affair it would seem...
New life empowers the land.

Awakening love releases the best.
Creation brought forth, birthed.
Stirring, harmonious unrest.
Drawing power, creation unearthed.

Newness of life, breath of fresh air.
Surrendering beauty revelations.
Brightness of colours, a joyous affair.
O Springtime permeates such a sensation

Song of Songs 4v16

Awake, north wind,
and come, south wind!
Blow on my garden,
that its fragrance may spread everywhere.
Let my beloved come into his garden
and taste its choice fruits.

RAINDROP

As the sunlight touches the raindrop,
hues of colour I do see.
Glistening rays of sparkling drops,
pure as can be.

Like falling gems from above,
so precious, yet so small.
Of great worth to us all.

Released from heaven above, they do fall.
Like liquid gold, so precious as a gem.
Raindrops from above, upon us do fall.
Sweet heavenly gift,
a rest and refreshing they do bring.

Within the raindrop is the seed of life.
Raindrops we sure do need.
From heaven they descend,
I believe God does them send.
Thank you for the heavenly gift.
Raindrops continue to flow.
Blessed be the little seeds, that they may grow!

Psalm 72v6

May he be like rain falling on a mown field,
like showers watering the earth.

WORSHIP LEADERS

Golden Scepter of Worship
Celestial abundance, Heavenly Worship.
Humble Beginnings, meek and mild.
Little child chasing butterflies.
Whispering love notes, harkened spirit.
Kingdom Realm upon you smiled.
Innocence your diadem.
Hidden treasure to be revealed.
Innermost being...drawn to more.
Succumbing to His Call.
Heavens Hands held you close.
Enriched spirit, pearls of praise.
Glorified and set apart.
New Beginnings, spiritual jewels within your veil.
Star of The Lord, shikinah from on High.
Upon your mouth He did kiss.
A seal set upon His Heart.
Sector of Worship, crowned minstrel of The Lord.
Sweet as honey, covenant worship, His vessel of praise.
Nova, all what God has called you to be.
Ever increasing...Sweet Manna.
Prophetic Revelator of worship.
Extraordinary Song of Songs as of old.
New Epistle Expression poured within.

The Sound of The Lord, chosen vessel.
Highly Exalted, Holy is Our Lord.
Redemption Song, rhythmic glory.
Manifest melody, cosmic echo.
Sing His Praises O Sing His Praises.
A Gift of Life...Exquisitely Revealed!
Selah (forever)

Isaiah 66v23

From one New Moon to another and from one Sabbath to another, all mankind will come and bow down before me

THE BROOK

A babbling brook I am,
definitely not a dam.
Along my way I chatter,
All day long I natter.

My water as clear as crystal.
I seem to keep in tune with a mistral.
Swishing along my way,
twirling, happy and gay.

Always happy and free.
I'm so glad to be me!
Having no time to waste,
I pick up my flow in haste.

Cascading through the meadow,
under the cherry tree's shadow.
Along my merry way I go,
I must continue in order to grow.

Sparkling water pure and sweet,
gushing forward, so much to meet.
There is much to consider,
to all forms of life I deliver

Proverbs 18v4

Wise words are like deep water; wisdom flows from the wise like a bubbling brook

MIGHTY TREE

I sat down in His shade.
It was a great delight.
Pondering all about this Tree,
gazing high above.
Through the branches I did see,
shimmering rays of pure sunlight.
I believe that in this Tree, God does delight.

From a little Seed, this Tree did grow.
I wonder who had a thought, and this
Seed sow.
In pure majesty He now stands.
Tall and strong, as sturdy as can be.
He towers above the lands.
How old are you Tree?
You seem to be so free!

You sway ever so lightly to and fro.
Yes, strong and sturdy though.
There is something about this Tree,
it has liberty and is free.

As I partake of the heavenly fruit,
so sweet to my taste.
Under His shadow I lay my head to rest.
Quietly I heard a whispering through the
leaves....
I heard that all that visit this Tree,

return to it's shade.
For in the whispering I heard....
THIS IS THE TREE THAT GOD MADE

Psalm 1v3

That person is like a tree planted by streams of
water,
which yields its fruit in season
and whose leaf does not wither—
whatever they do prospers.

VARIED INTIMACY

Multifarious divine intimacy
Varied shades of love
Born from deeper commitment
Ever growing in loving abidance

Spiritual dimensions of intimacy
Varied degrees of value
Transcending encompassing passion
Permeates being, deep within

Maturing love in intimacy
Varied keys of glory
Cascades, by covenant promise
Desire, drawn by attraction

Passion, the essence of intimacy
Varied vastness of manifold love
Fervent desire to draw closer
Blessed consummation of Spirit, Body and Soul

1 Corinthians 13v13

And now these three remain: faith, hope and love. But the greatest of these is love.

Song of Songs 6v2

*My beloved has gone down to his garden,
to the beds of spices,
to browse in the gardens
and to gather lilies.*

WONDERFUL LIGHT

Shining all around,
without even a sound.
Picture perfect rays,
brighten up my days.

Hues of colourful light.
Beaming with all its might.
Faceted realm of gold,
Poured from His hand, glowing bold.

Unveiling beautiful creation.
Revealing secrets of passion.
Sun of Righteousness.
Arise, behold His brightness.

Sun does clothe me well.
Encompassing light, in His presence I dwell.
Revelations of true beauty around.
Light reveals what is not yet found.

O' Brighten up my day,
In your embrace I love to stay.
Dancing rays from above,
The Light of the world is my love

2 Corinthians 4 v 6

For God, who said, "Let light shine out of darkness," a made his light shine in our hearts to give us the light of the knowledge of God's glory displayed in the face of Christ.

SIGNIFICANT

Clothed within a royal cocoon of gold.
Trapped by darkness, so cold.
Captured in stillness, haven of quietness.
Transformation of gentle life begins.

Manifest Godly power unseen.
Faith inherit, the struggle begins.
Long suffering, with grace, life unfolds,
turmoil deepens, enhanced mystery untold.

Growing from unsightly insignificance,
a hideous creature metamorphosis.
Caught up in transformation,
latent power begins to awake.

Gold clad fibers tense,
the mold begins to expand.
Struggle of life revealed,
beauty from ashes, breaks free.

Hallowed new birth on display.
Creational glory, personified.
Beautiful majestic butterfly,
robed in colourful righteousness.

Glistening silvery wings, outstretched.
Gold dusted body, her inheritance.

Now light be her redeemer, freed from the tomb.
Open sky, friendship, they joyfully embrace!

Significant...Overcomer of death

OCEAN

O Divine ocean so vast,
holds many a secret from the past.
Mystery flows within her wake.
Manifest beauty constantly the land rake.

O Body of ocean water,
veins of currents as strong as mortar.
Watery soul, generations does feed,
Many a mouth into her leads.

Accumulating power, encompassing the land,
'raging waves war, when she becomes mad.
Magnified authority within her belly holds,
Unravelling awakenings silently unfolds.

O Ocean beauty, why do you roar?
Even when seagulls above you do soar.
O Kingdom of water, your offspring you kindle,
Multitudes of life within you mingle.

Pacified beauty you are,
Reaching out, east to west, so far.
Ever so blue, majestic in reign.
Enthroned ocean, magnified domain,
God did you sincerely, ordain

Psalm 72 v 8

*May he rule from sea to sea
and from the River b to the ends of the earth.*

SUNFLOWERS

Swaying in the wind like an orchestra,
in time with the conductor.
A sea of sunflowers gaze to the sun.
Glowing yellow petals adorn their edges,
like a gown of splendid glory.

The first morning rays shine forth,
beaming faces turn to be kissed by the first
morning light.
An unfolding story begins,
and the wind sets into motion a soft note.
Whispering songs of peace.
A waltz of love, a whispering song,
sigh in a joy that sweeps the field.

They dance in tune with the Masters radiance.
His Light shines forth, and in the noon
day sun
a harvest of blaze exudes the glory of God.
A story of love unfolds, an afternoon tale
sings praises.

A sweep of butterflies glide by, dashing to
and fro.
O, what a harmony of royal flowers
being led by the hand of their King.
In the cool of the day a sweet scent
kisses the air and little ones tuck in for the night.

All by the guidance of the great, I AM.
The shadow of his wing swoops over
His blanket of love clothes them,
till the first peep of sunlight

Psalm 113 v 3

*From the rising of the sun to the place where
it sets,
the name of the Lord is to be praised.*

CASCADING LOVE

The love of God far surpasses our understanding.
His love is like rich oil poured forth,
illuminating radiance,
sparkling freshness.
As the morning dew, twinkling brilliance
with the first ray of light.
Golden ambience extended out.
A royal scepter of majestic glory.
His love encircles us as a gentle breeze,
scented with rich spices.
His wind of love caresses our hearts,
with a gentle touch, kisses our cheeks.
His love refreshes our being,
bubbling over revealing fruitful notes.
As a sweet champagne flowing over.
Cascading into a river of goodness, and knowing that,
God loves you

Psalm 40 v 16

But may all who seek you
rejoice and be glad in you;
may those who long for your saving help always say,
"The Lord is great!"

THE SEED

Planted deep beneath the earth,
hidden and out of sight.
In my turmoil, I need to birth,
and push towards the light.

Now just a tiny seed,
I do the light need.
In the womb of the earth,
my stature begins to grow.
A strength within begins to well.
By this I burst forth and begin to swell.

IT is so dark but warm down here.
Out of my husk I do break forth.
My vision is toward the North.
Through the earth I do push.
In my struggle there is a hush.

Tis my season to grow strong.
By God's Hand, I know He will help me along.
For I know what I will be...
not a vine, nor a stalk, but a mighty tree.

I can hear creation call, O nature.
That I into a mighty stature may mature.
Out of the shadowy depths...
I break free,
to become that mighty tree

Matthew 13 v 37

*He answered, "The one who sowed the good seed
is the Son of Man.*

FIRE

Colours of passion, bold and strong.
Raging heartless soul, boasts a song.
Devouring all within its path,
hungry untamed fire, kindled wrath.

Enchanting dance, O captivating motion,
hypnotizing all by its fiery emotion.
Fiery eyes ablaze, bent on destruction,
to consume and devour in order to function.

Scorching heat with ravishing kisses,
prancing flames, divining with hisses.
Giants of the woods cannot withstand the power.
Searing heat having ravishing tongues, O frenzied shower.

Delegated authority, crown of fire,
manifests its devious glorified attire.
Waves of ecstasy, who can it tame?
Embers remain as remnants of the flame

Psalm 78 v 14

*He guided them with the cloud by day
and with light from the fire all night.*

THE SOUND

O the Sound of Creation
Beckons the earth
Harkens untimely action
'O bring forth and birth.'

Breakthrough O little ones
The summons has begun
Behold O soul of nature yearns
Begin your upward call unto the Sun

Mysteries, unusual yet unique
Bold faith, unravelling divine
Unto the Sound does seek
The call of nature, 'They are Mine.'

Holy stirring in the sphere
Expectancy stirs in the air
Creation's Heart, O pondering Seer
Natures buoyant affair

Struggling ceases from deep within
Natures wisdom, paved with love
Bonded extravaganza, all akin
Beauty overshadowed from above

O The Sound of Creation
From on High You call
Winter, Summer, Spring and Fall
Patterns, in sync, gifts to all nations

The Spirit of Your Excellence forever shall be
The Sound of Creation, the call 'to be free! '

Whoever the Son sets free, is free indeed

Hebrews 2 v 12

"I will declare your name to my brothers and sisters;
in the assembly I will sing your praises."

WISDOM

Wisdom exudes from her lips.
Rich fragrance of knowledge and understanding.
Clothes as a garment of gold.
None can be compared to her.

Wisdom is all love.
Bountiful royal treasures,
within her bosom lies deep.
She extends out on compassionate wings.

Wisdom has an aroma, seal of presence.
Encompass O' wisdom, we seek after you.
Out of the secret place,
extraction of true beauty.

Wisdom is pure linen,
flowing royal colours.
She lifts the veil,
knowledge comes forth.

Wisdom may you feed us,
embrace us with your arms.
Harken our ears to hear.
Crown us with revelations.

Wisdom, you are fruitful, perfected.
A dawn of a new day,
all majestic in power and glory.
You hold the scales of righteousness.

Wisdom, poured with love,
encircled by gold.
Enriched with majestic beauty.
Upon her throne, forever.

Spirit of Her Excellence

Psalm 104 v 24

How many are your works, Lord!
In wisdom you made them all;
the earth is full of your creatures.

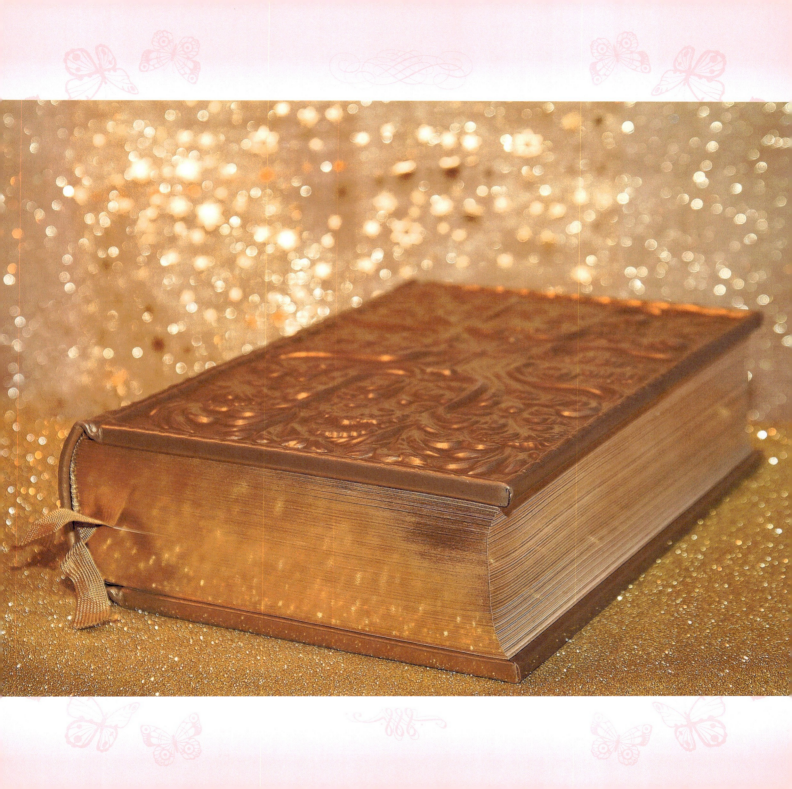

CREATION'S SONG

Colourful ribbons of life
Flowing magnificent rhythm
Golden waves of encompassing glory
Capturing creation's prophetic song.

God's canvas vividly displayed
His rythmic, spiritual paint brush flows freely
Expressions of harmony, manifest aglow
The melody of heaven, echoes from heart.

Creation's realistic show being told
Join the cosmic dance of joy
Golden seeds, redemptions harvest
Insync patterned story of God's best.

Knitted buds to multicoloured robed flowers
Sounds of creation ring out
Liberty of life brings forth
Out the abundance of the Almighty

Angels release creational promises from His treasury
Reign of blessings flow freely
Stoke the fire of pure delight
The gift of life exquisitely revealed!

Creation eagerly awaits for the revealing of the sons of God.

Psalm 98 v 10

Sing to the LORD a new song, for he has done marvelous things; his right hand and his holy arm have worked salvation for him.

SWEET COVENANT

His embrace, better than wine.
My inner being, entwined.
Precious oil poured forth,
soaked in His presence, He is mine.

Pleasant aroma fills the air,
sweet passion, a heavenly affair.
Closer, He draws me near.
No other love can compare.

Encompassing affection,
ever growing perfection.
Serene, delicate, His heart of love.
Drawn by His protection.

Our covenant ever so strong,
woven intricately together.
A harmonious bond forever.
Unto Him I will surrender.

I am my Beloved's, and He is mine

Psalm 111 v 9

He provided redemption for his people; he ordained his covenant forever-- holy and awesome is his name.

HEAVENLY WOMAN

O Woman, My rare and special treasures, uniquely fashioned.
Vessels of love, no man can measure.
Fruits of the Spirit, interwoven character beyond comprehension!
Sparkling jewels of faceted glory. Her value, a pearl of Great Worth.
O fountain of efficacy...your prayers move heaven and earth.

O Woman, your heart is set on faithfulness.
Upon The Rock you stand.
Around your head the diadem of fruitfulness.
Your Peace is found within His Heart.
Loyalty is unto her King, her offerings unto His Feet shall bring.

O Woman, An unfailing prize, her contribution moves the gates.
Royal garments, blue purple and red, fashioned dyes.
New Covenant spiritual attributes, upon The Lord she waits.
A spring of goodness, mission born out of selflessness.
O well of virtue! You are altogether mysterious...
In you there is always forgiveness.

O Woman, My fountain of joy! May I say, pure in heart.
Skillfully molded chambers within,
Hidden places that birth his word...too impart.

O Woman of inspiring Spirit
Pouring into vessels with whom she visits,
Always before her, the table of provision.
Humility is her blanket, humbleness of heart His extension.
She provides a pattern for her household,

Discipline, set upon Godly foundations.
Within the walls of her dwelling place, behold,
The all of kin grow in statue, overshadowed by passion.

O woman, a bouquet of dreams.
Your vision is set upon the upward call,
At times life is not always 'peaches and cream'.
Yet Ye persevere, with a sigh in faith…you always The Word recall.
Eager attitude, reconciliation always in mind.
In daily walk, within The Lord entwined.
Blessed is she, polished and refined!

O Woman, you have a taste for success.
In one thing…being confident in her Christ.
My desire is for all too succeed, have you not learned the game of Chess?
I have placed a Seed within you too progress,
Even the enemies gates you shall possess!
Weapons of war, so prophesy! I have paid the price.

O Woman, your diligence not unseen.
From morning dawn to late night hours.
Even in the merry-go-round of life, you are my queen!
Dusk to dawn you seek, even in your gardening My Face within the flowers you see.
Cool of the night, all tucked in,
Warm in my embrace, comforted within My Refuge Tower.

O Woman, Helping hand when in need.
Mercy clothes you, The choicest Robe.
My garments clothe your personality, set and guaranteed.
Freedom is in my raiment, closets of kaleidoscope.
Double portion inheritance, in preparation lies my blessings.
Your cup runneth over, rewards for perseverance.
Take heart my beloved, press into My New Beginnings!

O Woman, Tapestry of my Beauty.
Your handiwork flows, fine linen and cloth,
Bold fabrics, colourful threads, royal yet dainty.
In the capacity of apparel, having heavenward vision,
Kingdom perspectives Brough forth.
She is creative within her industry, able to set her hand to all profession.
Providing trade within her field, up to a hundredfold yield!
Testimony giver...I smile upon her expression!

O Woman, my crowning chorus, with all joy she sings praises,
Worship is her crown, in the breath of voice, her old's song amaze.
Wrapped in covenant relationship, clothed by my Gown.
My sweet-smelling fragrance, bathed in richest of oil spices.
Her faith, heavenly aroma, strong in elegance.
Blow O North Wind, so the scents arise!

Her Reward is with her, The Harvest ever before. Looking unto the restoration of all things,
She is my joy and crown, a woman of substance. Upon her lips there is prayer, supplication
And praise. She ponders upon whatsoever is pure, lovely and things of good report.
Psalm 45:13 The Kings Daughter is all glorious within, her clothing is of gold!

I beseech you O Daughters of Zion, Worship Him, Worship God!

Selah

Proverbs 31

HEAVENLY FRAGRANCE

Fragrance of Life
a heavenly affair.
Oriental perfume captivates
the essence of all.

Flowing in abundance,
sensual aroma scents the air.
Sweet smelling fragrance,
arises in glory, praises on high.

Ancient of spices, richly bases oils.
Royal perfume gladly sent.
Swirling sweet savor,
anointing freshness, quickens the senses.

Fragrance of blessing, pure oil of joy.
Varied ingredients, interwoven surprise.
Choicest of all, form the mountain of spices.
Manifest fragrance, encompassing glory.

Heavenly fragrance released from above.
Anointing oil, cinnamon, saffron, myrrh, to
name a few.
Swirling creation, dancing sweet fragrance.
Life's sweet blessings, awakens the Spirit.

Come to the garden of Heavenly Fragrance

Song of Solomon 4 v 16

Awake, north wind,
and come, south wind!
Blow on my garden,
that its fragrance may spread everywhere.
Let my beloved come into his garden
and taste its choice fruits.

A ROSE

All my petals did lay all around,
scattered about on the ground.
Suffering through brokenness.
Until He did me found.

One by one He did mend,
Did for me the heaven rend.
Now I begin to take shape,
my inner being awakes.

Kisses upon me He does blow.
Captivated I blossom, beginning to glow.
Sweet perfume fills the room,
as if I were a bride, meeting her Groom.

By His hand I have been made whole,
the upward call, is my goal.
Happy I am, the rose within His hand.
Held together by His Trinity band.

All my petals perfect in array,
to His tune I do sway.
Swept up by His love for me.
Now I am whole...
His seal of love,
a perfect guarantee

Song of Songs 2 v 1

I am a rose of Sharon, a lily of the valleys.

STARS

Harmony of stars, they do sing.
Twinkling beauties of the realm.
Sparkling cosmic diamonds,
creations glittering diadem.

Held by the celestial cord.
Creations song, glorifies faith.
Brightening up the darkest of sky.
Scattered beauties, blown from God's hand.

Varied size and shape, biggest to smallest,
all have an angelic tune.
Stars of the heaven, so divine,
shining majestic gems, of the night sky.

They sing a song of unity,
part of God's treasure chest revealed.
Shekinah glory, iridescent display.
Heavenly beauties, unto us do wink

Psalm 147 v 4

*He determines the number of the stars
and calls them each by name.*

THE END IS JUST THE BEGINNING

The End is Just The Beginning!

Clothed within a chamber of gloom. Trapped by darkness, so cold.

Captured in torture, mocked and scorned.

O crown of thorns, does sting. Transformation of All sin.

Devouring untamed fire, devious wrath. Encroached power of darkness, intent to seal its mark.

The sixth hour, darkness came. Manifest stealth, encircling, capturing grief.

The gates of Hades could not stand! All Authority born from His Body, O manifold crown of deceit…

Your kingdom keys revoked, you have been beat!

Unsightly Significance, caught up in Transformation! Power awakened, grave clothes expand. Beauty from ashes breaks forth!

Hallowed Resurrection, creations Glory.

Personified, Majesty, robed in Righteousness.

Our Redeemer Arisen!

Light of the World put darkness under His Feet.

Son of Righteousness…Behold His Brightness!

By the Cross we have been made whole. Held together by His Trinity Band, a seal of Love, an Exquisite Guarantee!!

Surely, I come Quickly

The Spirit and The Bride say " Come"! Selah

Hebrew 12 v 2

Looking unto Jesus the author and finisher of our faith; who for the joy that was set before him endured the cross, despising the shame, and is set down at the right hand of the throne of God.

any people in the crowds, however, who believe...
nen the Christ comes, will he give more signs...
ours like this about him were spreading among...
ent the Temple police to arrest him.

aid:
ll remain with you for only a short time now;
I shall go back to the one who sent me.
will look for me and will not find me:
e I am
cannot come.'

en said to one another, 'Where is he going...
m? Is he going abroad to the people who...
will he teach the Greeks? What does he mean...
u will look for me and will not find me:
re I am,
cannot come"?'

of living water

day and greatest day of the festival, Jesus st...
any man is thirsty, let him come to me!
the man come and drink who believes in m...
ays: From his breast shall flow fountains of living water.
eaking of the Spirit which those who believed in him were to receiv...
no Spirit as yet because Jesus had not yet been glorified.

ions on the origin of the Messiah

ople who had been listening said, 'Surely he must be the prophet'
id, 'He is the Christ', but others said, 'Would the Christ be from...
es not scripture say that the Christ must be descended from David...
om the town of Bethlehem?' So the people could not agree about...
would have liked to arrest him, but no one actually laid hands on...

ce went back to the chief priests and Pharisees who said to them,
't you brought him?' The police replied, 'There has never been...
o has spoken like him'. So the Pharisees answered 'you have been...
s well? Have any of the authorities believed in him? Any of the...
This rabble knows nothing about the Law—they are damned...
n, Nicodemus—the same man who had come to Jesus earlier—said...
surely the Law does not allow us to pass judgement on a man without...
a hearing and discovering what he is about?' To this they answered...
Galilean too? Go into the matter, and see for yourself: prophets do...
ut of Galilee.'

ous woman"

went home, 8 and Jesus went to the Mount of Olives.
reak he appeared in the Temple again; and as all the people came...
own and began to teach them.
brought a woman along who had been...
stand there in full view...

the light of the world

When Jesus spoke to the people again, he said:
'I am the light of the world;
anyone who follows me will not be walking in the dark;
he will have the light of life'.

testimony of Jesus to himself

At this the Pharisees said to him, 'You are testifying on your own beha...
is not valid'. Jesus replied:

'It is true that I am testifying on my own behalf,
but my testimony is still valid,
because I know where I came from and where I am going;
but you do not know where I come from or where I am going.
You judge by human standards;
I judge no one,

THE END

My poetry is a brush, my words are the paint! Reveal my words O Lord...to paint pictures for all too see. Amen

Psalm 45:1

Beautiful words stir my heart. I will recite a lovely poem about the king, for my tongue is like the pen of a skillful poet.

Isaiah 45:3

And I will give you the treasures of darkness and hidden riches of secret places, that you may know I the Lord, calls you by name.

May God our Father and the Lord Jesus Christ give you grace and peace. Amen (Selah)

Printed in the United States
By Bookmasters